Put Beginning Readers on the Right Track with
ALL ABOARD READING™

The All Aboard Reading series is especially designed for beginning readers. Written by noted authors and illustrated in full color, these are books that children really want to read—books to excite their imagination, expand their interests, make them laugh, and support their feelings. With fiction and nonfiction stories that are high interest and curriculum-related, All Aboard Reading books offer something for every young reader. And with four different reading levels, the All Aboard Reading series lets you choose which books are most appropriate for your children and their growing abilities.

Picture Readers

Picture Readers have super-simple texts, with many nouns appearing as rebus pictures. At the end of each book are 24 flash cards—on one side is a rebus picture; on the other side is the written-out word.

Station Stop 1

Station Stop 1 books are best for children who have just begun to read. Simple words and big type make these early reading experiences more comfortable. Picture clues help children to figure out the words on the page. Lots of repetition throughout the text helps children to predict the next word or phrase—an essential step in developing word recognition.

Station Stop 2

Station Stop 2 books are written specifically for children who are reading with help. Short sentences make it easier for early readers to understand what they are reading. Simple plots and simple dialogue help children with reading comprehension.

Station Stop 3

Station Stop 3 books are perfect for children who are reading alone. With longer text and harder words, these books appeal to children who have mastered basic reading skills. More complex stories captivate children who are ready for more challenging books.

In addition to All Aboard Reading books, look for All Aboard Math Readers™ (fiction stories that teach math concepts children are learning in school); All Aboard Science Readers™ (nonfiction books that explore the most fascinating science topics in age-appropriate language); All Aboard Poetry Readers™ (funny, rhyming poems for readers of all levels); and All Aboard Mystery Readers™ (puzzling tales where children piece together evidence with the characters).

All Aboard for happy reading!

To my relatives and ancestors from Romania,
the Branzei and Ardelean families. Maybe there
was a vampire or two.—S.B.

GROSSET & DUNLAP
Published by the Penguin Group
Penguin Group (USA) Inc., 375 Hudson Street, New York, New York 10014, USA
Penguin Group (Canada), 90 Eglinton Avenue East, Suite 700, Toronto,
Ontario M4P 2Y3, Canada (a division of Pearson Penguin Canada Inc.)
Penguin Books Ltd., 80 Strand, London WC2R 0RL, England
Penguin Group Ireland, 25 St. Stephen's Green, Dublin 2, Ireland
(a division of Penguin Books Ltd.)
Penguin Group (Australia), 250 Camberwell Road, Camberwell, Victoria 3124,
Australia (a division of Pearson Australia Group Pty. Ltd.)
Penguin Books India Pvt. Ltd., 11 Community Centre, Panchsheel Park,
New Delhi—110 017, India
Penguin Group (NZ), 67 Apollo Drive, Rosedale, North Shore 0632, New Zealand
(a division of Pearson New Zealand Ltd.)
Penguin Books (South Africa) (Pty.) Ltd., 24 Sturdee Avenue,
Rosebank, Johannesburg 2196, South Africa

Penguin Books Ltd., Registered Offices:
80 Strand, London WC2R 0RL, England

Text copyright © 2009 by Sylvia Branzei. Illustrations copyright © 2009 by Jack Keely.
All rights reserved. Published by Grosset & Dunlap, a division of Penguin Young Readers
Group, 345 Hudson Street, New York, New York 10014. ALL ABOARD READING and
GROSSET & DUNLAP are trademarks of Penguin Group (USA) Inc.
Printed in the U.S.A.

Library of Congress Cataloging-in-Publication Data

Branzei, Sylvia.
Ickstory : the history of vampires and other real blood drinkers / by Sylvia Branzei ;
illustrations by Jack Keely.
p. cm.
ISBN 978-0-448-45032-2 (pbk.)
1. Vampires--Juvenile literature. I. Keely, Jack. II. Title.
BF1556.B73 2009
398'.45--dc22
2008022295

ISBN 978-0-448-45032-2   10 9 8 7 6 5 4 3 2 1

ALL ABOARD READING™

Station Stop
3

ICKSTORY

An Icky, Sticky
History of the World

The History of

VAMPIRES

and Other Real Blood Drinkers

by Sylvia Branzei   illustrated by Jack Keely

Do you know what blood tastes like?

Imagine a cup of warm blood. Stick your finger in the cup. What does it feel like? Is it sticky and goopy, like tomato soup? Or is it lumpy, like oatmeal?

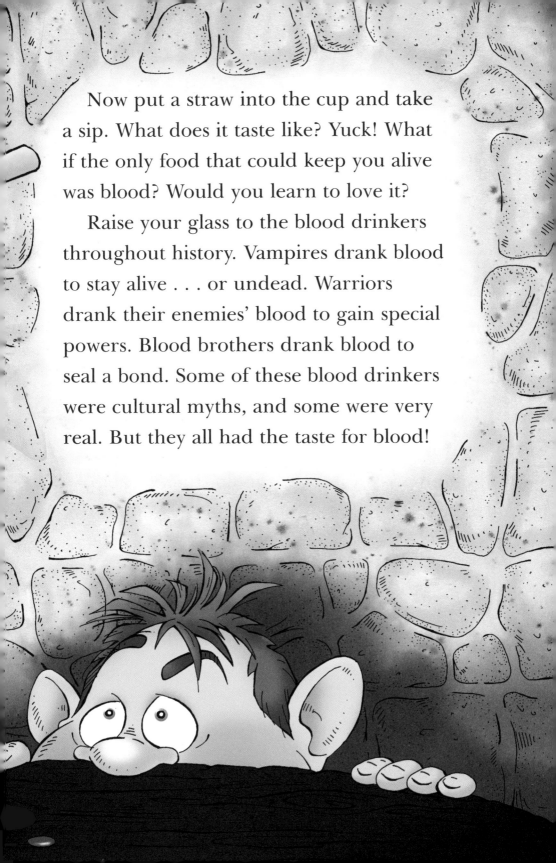

Now put a straw into the cup and take a sip. What does it taste like? Yuck! What if the only food that could keep you alive was blood? Would you learn to love it?

Raise your glass to the blood drinkers throughout history. Vampires drank blood to stay alive . . . or undead. Warriors drank their enemies' blood to gain special powers. Blood brothers drank blood to seal a bond. Some of these blood drinkers were cultural myths, and some were very real. But they all had the taste for blood!

CHAPTER 1
Blood-slurping Bats

What do you think is more disgusting: drinking someone else's blood or barfing into your friend's mouth? Guess what—vampire bats do both!

All bats are furry and have wings, but only one group of bats has very sharp teeth— vampire bats. These razor-sharp fangs help vampire bats get dinner—blood. Vampire bats also have heat sensors in their noses that help them find the best selection of blood possible. *Sniff, sniff, chomp.*

Vampire bats hang upside down in the caves of Central and South America. During the day, they sleep. But in the middle of the night, vampire bats leave the cave. *Flap, flap, flap.*

Picture this: A vampire bat silently lands on the back of a horse sleeping in its corral. The bat searches around, then licks the perfect spot on the horse's back. The bat's fangs slice into the animal's skin like a sharp knife. The blood oozes from the wound as the bat's saliva keeps the horse's blood flowing.

Each night a vampire bat sips a spoonful of blood. Over the course of one year, one vampire bat will drink about five-and-a-half liters of blood. A group of 100 blood-sucking bats could drain all the blood from 13 cows!

But drinking
an animal's blood is
nothing special, right?
Even a mosquito can do
that! What really
separates the vampire
bats from the ordinary
bloodsucking creatures is this:
Back at the cave a well-fed bat will
gladly vomit into the mouth of a hungry
roost-mate. "Hungry? Here you go! *Raaaalf.*"
The exchange looks kind of like kissing, only
they are really swapping bloody barf. Want some?

MARCH

Vampire bats drink cow blood, horse blood, chicken blood, sheep blood, goat blood, pig blood, duck blood, and human blood. Yes, they will sometimes drink human blood. That doesn't happen very often though, so don't be afraid to sleep outside! But imagine what it would be like if vampire bats did drink human blood: If you woke up to find a V-shaped cut on your finger, big toe, or ear, you might think a vampire bat stole your blood while you were cozy and snuggled up, asleep in dreamland!

CHAPTER 2
The Most Famous Bloodsucker of Them All

Name the most famous bloodsucker you can think of. You probably said, "Dracula, of course," right? You have a good reason to say Dracula . . . because he is everywhere. Dracula appears in movies and on television shows. He sells cereal and candy. He even teaches kids how to count! He is so popular that most people never even think about what he does. He drinks human blood!

Imagine this: You're asleep in your bed as Dracula wanders the streets. Suddenly, he spots you asleep in your bed. He turns into a bat and flies into the bedroom. He leans over the bed with his mouth open wide and chomps into your neck. Dracula feasts on the blood. Then he escapes.

You can try to keep an eye out for him,
but Dracula can make himself blend into a
normal crowd. He is tall with dark hair and
pale skin. He is always dressed in
evening clothes and a black cloak.
He usually looks like a regular
person. Well, except for his fangs.
That's always a dead giveaway . . .

13

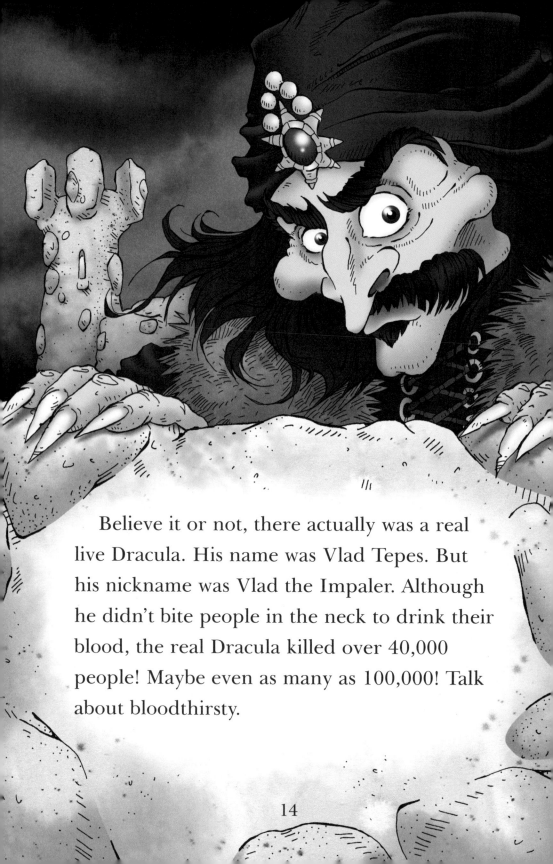

Believe it or not, there actually was a real live Dracula. His name was Vlad Tepes. But his nickname was Vlad the Impaler. Although he didn't bite people in the neck to drink their blood, the real Dracula killed over 40,000 people! Maybe even as many as 100,000! Talk about bloodthirsty.

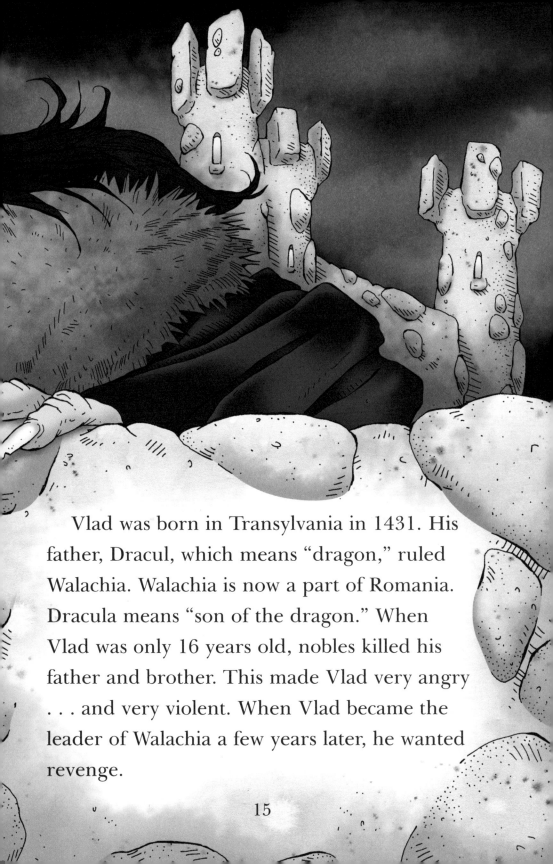

Vlad was born in Transylvania in 1431. His
father, Dracul, which means "dragon," ruled
Walachia. Walachia is now a part of Romania.
Dracula means "son of the dragon." When
Vlad was only 16 years old, nobles killed his
father and brother. This made Vlad very angry
. . . and very violent. When Vlad became the
leader of Walachia a few years later, he wanted
revenge.

As soon as Vlad returned to Walachia, he threw a big party. He invited all of the nobles from the land to attend. (These were the same people who killed his father and brother.) The nobles brought their families. They feasted and laughed with Dracula for many hours. But at the end of the night, Vlad didn't send his guests home with party favors. Instead, he arrested them.

Dracula impaled the older nobles and their families. Impaling is when you push a sharp stake through a person's body. *Ouch!* But this was just the beginning of Dracula's terror.

Impaling became one of Dracula's favorite methods of killing people. Sometimes he arranged the stakes in circles around the city. Sometimes he left them for months to rot. Ever smell food rotting in the garbage? It got pretty stinky. However, it worked to keep his enemies away.

Sometimes, Dracula dined in the forest filled with these dead bodies. One day in 1459, he invited the nobles for a feast in the "Forest of the Impaled." The nobles didn't want to come, but what else could they do? Nobody wanted to stand up to their scary ruler.

An author named Bram Stoker was so fascinated by Dracula that he wrote a book about him in 1897! Bram Stoker based his fictional character on the real Vlad Dracula. There were a lot of similarities between the two. In his book, Count Dracula is a nobleman who owns a castle in Transylvania. He moves to England in search of fresh blood. But when he gets hunted down, he flees back to his castle. Someone finally captures him and kills Count Dracula once and for all.

Bram Stoker knew a whole lot about vampires by the time he finished writing his book. But before writing the book, he spent seven years studying vampire legends. What other vampires and vampire legends could he have studied?

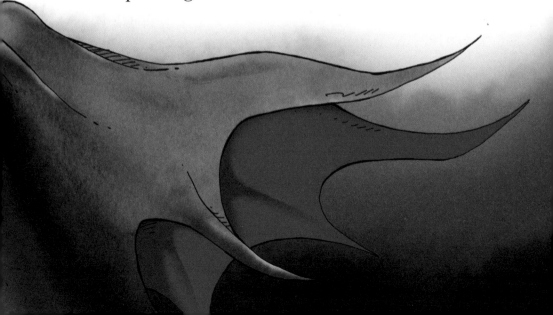

CHAPTER 3
A Taste for Blood

Vampires are dead bodies that come back to life. The undead can be almost any sort of animal, especially a bat. But mostly, the undead are humans who wander at night in search of blood. Just like Dracula, many vampires prefer human blood.

Almost every country around the world has myths about vampires. Myths are stories. They are not real. Here are some myths whispered through the ages about vampires who haunt and hunt the living.

Lamia is a Greek vampire. She is
a woman on the top half of her body
and a snake on the bottom half. Lamia
can never close her eyes. However, she can
remove her eyeballs. After a long night of
bloodsucking, Lamia just pops out her eyes.

Jiang Shi are Chinese. (You pronounce their name "gyon shee.") They don't actually suck blood. Instead they suck the life out of people. They are bright green with many sharp teeth and long claws. They don't walk. They hop. If you see a Jiang Shi hopping toward you, hold your breath. They are blind, so if you're not breathing, they won't hear you. They will *hop, hop, hop* right by you.

Manananggals are Filipino bloodsuckers. The word *manananggal* is a mouthful. It means "one who separates itself from its lower body." A manananggal is usually a woman during the day. At night, the top half of her body sprouts wings and separates from the bottom half.

The half-bodied woman flies around and
lands on the roof of a house. She sucks the
blood out of unsuspecting victims that are
inside the house.

A Yara-Ma-Yha-Who lives in the fig
trees of Australia. It is about four feet tall.
This vampire is red, with a large toothless
mouth, a very large head,
and suction cups on the tips
of its fingers and toes.

When the Yara-Ma-Yha-Who sees a person at the bottom of his tree, it drops down to the ground. Then it drains the blood out of the victim using the suckers on its fingers and toes. The person becomes very weak, but he doesn't die. The Yara-Ma-Yha-Who then opens its large mouth and swallows the person whole! *Gulp!* It does a dance, drinks some water, and falls asleep. The Yara-Ma-Yha-Who then wakes up and vomits out the entire meal. Usually the person is still alive. The best thing to do if you are caught by a Yara-Ma-Yha-Who is go along with the whole thing. When the creature vomits you out, run away really fast.

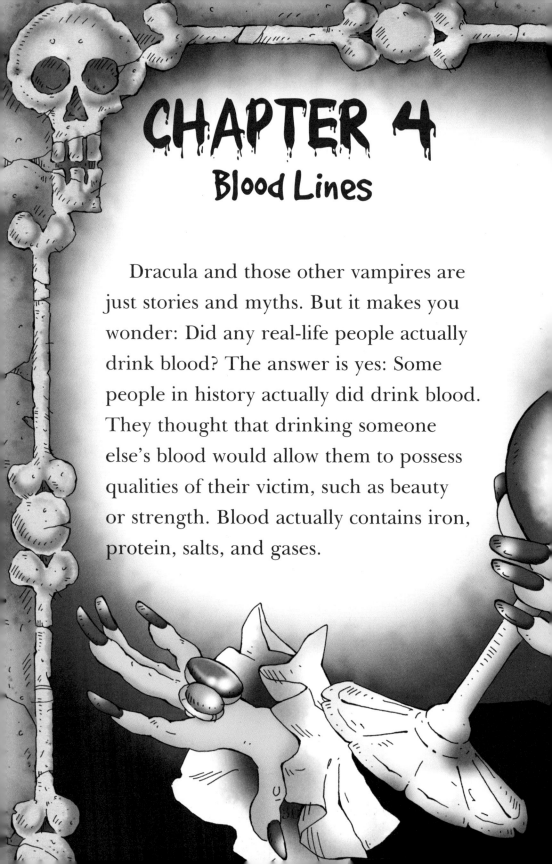

CHAPTER 4
Blood Lines

Dracula and those other vampires are just stories and myths. But it makes you wonder: Did any real-life people actually drink blood? The answer is yes: Some people in history actually did drink blood. They thought that drinking someone else's blood would allow them to possess qualities of their victim, such as beauty or strength. Blood actually contains iron, protein, salts, and gases.

Elizabeth Bathory was a wealthy countess who lived in Hungary during the 1600s. Elizabeth Bathory is also known as the Blood Countess and the Blood Lady of Cachtice. The names suit her very well.

The story goes that one day a maid accidentally pulled the countess's hair while combing it. Elizabeth slapped the girl so hard, blood landed on her hand. The countess noticed the blood made her skin smooth and young. So rumors say that she began to drain the blood from young women to bathe in it. Some stories add that she drank the blood to give herself inner beauty.

It is rumored that she killed 600 girls to get the blood she needed. But Elizabeth did not act alone. Her servants helped her. The countess poked holes into a girl's skin to make the blood *drip, drip, drip.*

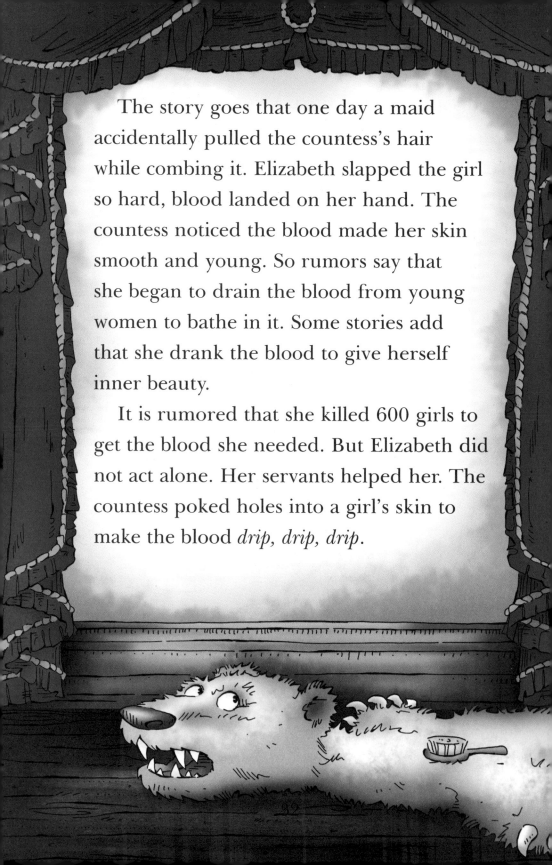

There is also a rumor that Elizabeth and her servants built a special device to make blood pour down on anyone standing below. Some people say Elizabeth would drink the blood, and some say she would just let it cover her.

After going through all of her servant girls,
Elizabeth Bathory decided it was time to go
for noble blood. Noble families sent their
daughters to the countess's finishing school.
And finish them she did! The families thought
their girls would learn about manners and
the ways of becoming a lady. Instead of being
trained, the girls were drained—of their blood.
Rumors began to spread.

The king ordered a raid on the castle. Soldiers searched and found about 50 bodies inside the castle. The countess was sentenced to stay in her bedroom for the rest of her life.

The Blood Countess wasn't the only one who drank blood to stay powerful and young. Tribal warriors wanted strength and power so they developed a blood-drinking ritual of their own. Legends tell that prisoners were marched onto a field. A Moche priest from Peru would cut the prisoners' necks. A priestess collected the gushing blood in a golden cup. The priestess handed the cup filled with warm blood to the priest. The priest lifted the golden goblet and drank the fresh blood.

Blood clots very easily. Luckily, the Moche discovered a local fruit called *ulluchu* that kept the blood from clumping. No one wants lumpy blood now, do they?

In the late 1800s, an English explorer witnessed a victory feast in New Zealand. He watched in horror as the Maori drank their enemy soldiers' blood.

It is believed that the Maori thought that the blood carried knowledge and living power from the dead person to the drinker. It was probably best to stay friends with these tribal people, don't you think?

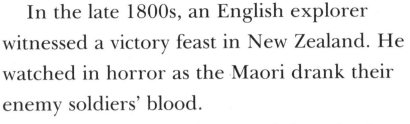

Like the Maori, the ancient Celts from Western Europe believed you could gain the power of your enemy by drinking their blood. They sipped their enemies' blood from a handy cup crafted from their enemies' skull.

But the Celts also drank blood from those they loved. The Celts thought this brought them closer to the dearly departed. Good qualities were also thought to be passed on through the blood. So, if your brother was smart and strong, you could also become smart and strong after drinking his blood. But if your brother was a brat, maybe you wouldn't want any of his blood.

From 100 to 400 CE, the Romans enjoyed watching gladiators fight beasts in an open arena. They often fought until death. The dead gladiator's blood was cherished. People believed it was magical, which is strange because it certainly wasn't very magical for the gladiator.

A sip of a gladiator's blood was also thought to cure diseases. The Romans thought diseases were a curse from the gods. One of the cures was a drink of magical gladiator's blood.

The Lydians lived several thousand years ago in what is now Turkey. They performed a special blood brother ceremony. Each person cut into his arm with a sharp object.

Then they licked the blood off each other's arms. Yuck. After this messy event, they were blood brothers. They were also very sticky.

The Scythians rode horses over Eastern Europe and Central Asia from 7th century BCE through 1st century BCE. Here is a recipe for blood brotherhood. (But don't try this yourself!)

Gather together a sharp knife, a cup, some wine, an arm, and a friend. Use the sharp knife to cut into your arm. Let your blood drip into the cup. Repeat for the future blood brother. Add a bit of wine into the glass. Stir the blood and wine mixture well. Drink, share, and enjoy.

Vampires are the undead who have come back to life to sip on blood. Vampires are mythical. There were probably no real vampires in history. But, the idea of an undead human waiting outside your bedroom to suck your blood is scary.

However, bloodthirsty nobles like Vlad Dracula and Countess Bathory existed in history. And even better, actual blood drinkers like vampire bats, warriors, and blood brothers also roamed free among the living. Long live Dracula and his friends!